Animal B

Monica Hughes

This baby can hug its mother.

This baby can hug too.

This baby can ride on its mother's back.

This baby can ride too.

This baby can hang on to its mother.

This baby can hang on too.

This baby can ride in its mother's pouch.

This baby can ride too.

This baby can hold on to its mother's fur.

This baby can hold on too.

This baby can hold on to its mother too!